# The WANTED

# CONTENTS

**Published By Century Books Limted,**
Unit I, Upside Station Building,
Solsbro Road, Torquay, Devon, TQ2 6FD.
books@centurybooksltd.co.uk   Published 2012.

Under license from Bravado Merchandising.
All rights reserved.

£7.99

# WE ARE...

Welcome to the official 2013 Annual of Britain's hottest boy band – bar none! Since bursting onto the scene in 2009, the guys have taken the UK by storm, notched up 3 sell-out tours and even succeeded in cracking the United States.

This essential annual is packed with everything you need to know about the fab five. There are facts, quizzes and inside goss. What are you waiting for? It's time to dive into the world of The Wanted...

# The WANTED

## BACKSTAGE PASS

FIRST NAME:

...................................

SURNAME:

...................................

DATE OF BIRTH:

...................................

AGE:

...................................

STICK A PICTURE OF YOURSELF IN HERE

MAX

The WANTED

8

# Fact file

**Full name:** Maximillian Alberto George
**Place of birth:** Manchester
**Date of birth:** 6th September 1988
**Star sign:** Virgo
**Eye colour:** Green/hazel
**Hair colour:** Dark brown (although according to Jay, "it's always shaved so could be ginger as far as we know!")

**Fave meal:** Full English breakfast
**Fave book:** *Jaws* by Peter Benchleys
**Musical heroes:** Elvis and Nat King Cole
**Greatest fear:** Losing people

## AND ANOTHER THING

Max is a qualified diver and has a major shark obsession. He would love to be a cage diver with sharks (including Great Whites) one day.

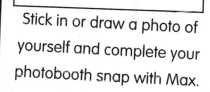

Stick in or draw a photo of yourself and complete your photobooth snap with Max.

## MAD ABOUT MAX ?

Then fill-in the phrases below to spell out why you connect with the sultry star.

Max rocks because ...........................................................................................
...........................................................................................................................
Max and I are similar because ......................................................................
...........................................................................................................................
If I could spend a day with Max we'd ...........................................................
...........................................................................................................................
I'd say ...............................................................................................................
...........................................................................................................................
I'd wear .............................................................................................................
...........................................................................................................................

## TOP 5 MOMENTS OF 2012 !

Meeting J-Lo on American Idol
City winning the league
Mario Balotelli
My brother getting his first credit on a film (Prometheus)
Partying with Scooter Braun

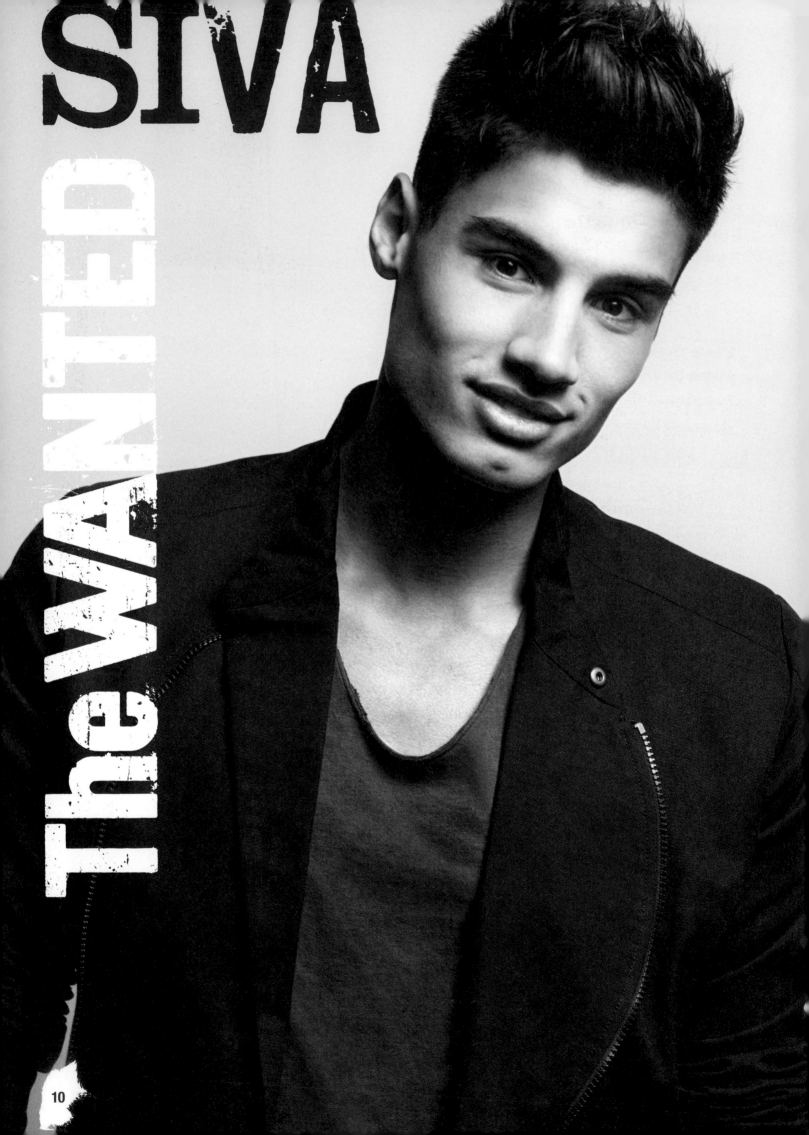

SIVA

The WANTED

# Fact file

| | |
|---|---|
| **Full name:** | Siva Kaneswaran |
| **Place of birth:** | Ireland |
| **Date of birth:** | 16th November 1988 |
| **Star sign:** | Scorpio |
| **Eye colour:** | Brown |
| **Hair colour:** | Black |
| **Fave meal:** | Roast |
| **Fave book:** | *Digital Fortress* by Dan Brown |
| **Musical heroes:** | Michael Jackson |
| **Greatest fear:** | Polka dots |

Stick in or draw a photo of yourself and complete your photobooth snap with Siva.

## AND ANOTHER THING

Half Irish, half Sri Lankan. Hair like Elvis, face like a sculpture in bronze. Jay describes Siva as "very down to Earth. Humble. Very creative. He also brings a sense of balance and culture."

## SWEET ON SIVA ?

…then fill in the phrases below to describe how you feel about the Irish beauty.

Siva rocks because................................................................................................
....................................................................................................................
Siva and I are similar because................................................................................
....................................................................................................................
If I could spend a day with Siva we'd ....................................................................
....................................................................................................................
I'd say ............................................................................................................
....................................................................................................................
....................................................................................................................
I'd wear ..........................................................................................................
....................................................................................................................

## TOP 5 MOMENTS OF 2012 !

Running with the Olympic torch
Final gig of The Code tour in Dublin
Travelling in New Zealand
Releasing 'I Found You'
Meeting the First Lady

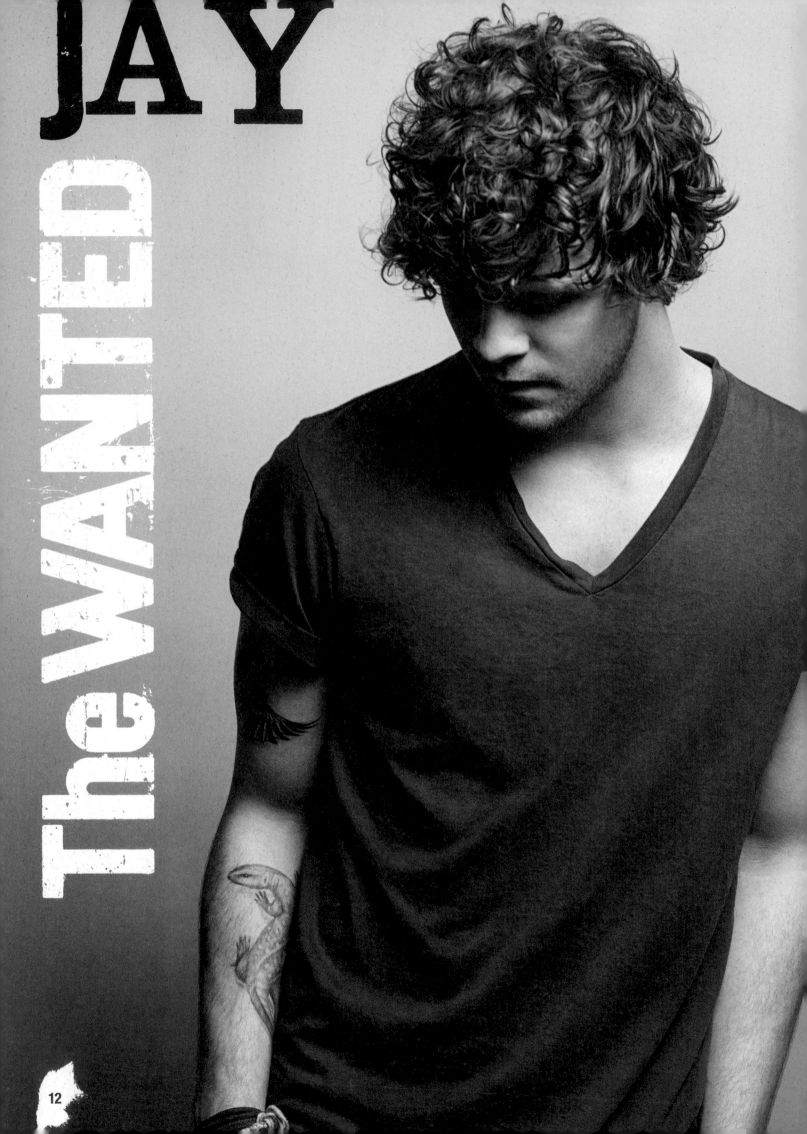

# Fact file

**Full name:** James Kevin McGuiness
**Place of birth:** Newark
**Date of birth:** 24th July 1990
**Star sign:** Leo
**Eye colour:** Blue
**Hair colour:** Brown
**Fave meal:** Vegetarian sushi
**Fave book:** *Bad Sciencee* by Ben Goldacre
**Musical heroes:** Cat Stevens, Newton Faulkner, Damien Rice
**Greatest fear:** Family and friends dying

Stick in or draw a photo of yourself and complete your photobooth snap with Jay.

## AND ANOTHER THING

Jay's got a steadily growing tattoo sleeve which features a compass, his lizard, oak leaves & a jay bird.

## JUST CRAZY FOR JAY?

…then fill in the phrases below to remind yourself why you can't get enough of the curly-haired cutie.

Jay rocks because ....................................................................................................
.................................................................................................................................

Jay and I are similar because......................................................................................
.................................................................................................................................

If I could spend a day with Jay we'd ..........................................................................
.................................................................................................................................

I'd say.........................................................................................................................
.................................................................................................................................
.................................................................................................................................

I'd wear .....................................................................................................................
.................................................................................................................................

## TOP 5 MOMENTS OF 2012 !

Me & my brothers birthday surprise party with all our friends
Deciding I like sweetcorn after all
My brother graduating from Uni
Running with the olympic torch and a questionably unfashionable bandana
The Moment when Holly from Jordy Shore threw up a scotch egg

# NATHAN

## The WANTED

# Fact file

**Full name:** Nathan James Sykes
**Place of birth:** Gloucester
**Date of birth:** 18th April 1993
**Star sign:** Aries
**Eye colour:** Greeny-blue
**Hair colour:** Brown
**Fave meal:** Spaghetti Bolognese, Chinese
**Fave book:** 50 Shades of Nathan
**Musical heroes:** Stevie Wonder, Boyz II Men, John Legend
**Greatest fear:** Exposed heights

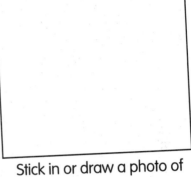

Stick in or draw a photo of yourself and complete your photobooth snap with Nathan.

## AND ANOTHER THING

Nathan loves getting into the studio and writing & producing new songs.

## NUTS ABOUT NATHAN ?

...then fill in the phrases below to describe how you feel about the baby of the band.

Nathan rocks because ..........................................................................................................

Nathan and I are similar because ............................................................................................

If I could spend a day with Nathan we'd .................................................................................

I'd say ........................................................................................................................

I'd wear ......................................................................................................................

## TOP 5 MOMENTS OF 2012 !

Performing at Wembley Stadium
My 19th Birthday party
Running with the torch
Performing at the Billboard Awards
Meeting Stevie Wonder

TOM

The WANTED

# Fact file

| | |
|---|---|
| **Full name:** | Thomas Anthony Parker |
| **Place of birth:** | Bolton |
| **Date of birth:** | 14th August 1988 |
| **Star sign:** | Leo |
| **Eye colour:** | Haze; |
| **Hair colour:** | Brown |
| **Fave meal:** | Indian, Italian |
| **Fave book:** | Crime books |
| **Musical heroes:** | Nirvana, Oasis |
| **Greatest fear:** | Heights |

Stick in or draw a photo of yourself and complete your photobooth snap with Tom.

## AND ANOTHER THING

Tom's a clever clogs! He earned a place on a degree course to study geography at Manchester Metropolitan University, but the lure of showbiz proved too strong!

## TOTALLY INTO TOM?

Then fill-in the phrases below to spell out why you connect with the rugged star.

Tom rocks because..................................................................................
.................................................................................................................

Tom and I are similar because ...............................................................
.................................................................................................................

If I could spend a day with Tom we'd ....................................................
.................................................................................................................

I'd say .......................................................................................................
.................................................................................................................
.................................................................................................................

I'd wear .....................................................................................................
.................................................................................................................

## TOP 5 MOMENTS OF 2012 !

Starting my own T-shirt company  #entrepreneur

Finding a sparrow in my sink

Harvesting Siva's grey hairs and making them into a pillow

Doing an amazing performance at a great school in Milwaukee

Watching Jordan Sparks perform 'I will Always Love You' at the Billboard Awards in tribute to Whitney Houston

# 2012 HG.

As part of their mission to break the States, the lads conducted a month-long promotional tour, stopping in at TV and radio stations around the country. The band conducted live interviews and wowed listeners with fab acoustic versions of their songs. No wonder the country fell for them.

"How do you spell Tom?"

Acoustic sesh.

Sightseeing at the Empire State in NYC

Thumbs up for the Ellen Show

Posing for the cameras

The boys also dropped in to do a live set for fans at 103.5 Kiss FM's Coca-Cola Lounge where the host quizzed them about their 'Ellen Show' appearance - they described Ellen as 'hot' and Max and Nathan melted hearts by admitting animal-related films make them cry.

Coca-Cola-tastic!

Signing up a storm

Wowing fans

## The Tonight Show with Jay Leno

When the guys played Jay Leno, adoring fans stormed the stage. Max positively welcomed the intrusion, beckoning them on stage and saying, "Come on, as many as you want… who's coming to Vegas with us tonight?"

Singing 'Glad You Came' on The Tonight Show with Jay Leno

Performing 'Chasing the Sun' on The Voice (US)

## MTV Spring Break

The party really got going in Las Vegas, when The Wanted dropped in to perform on MTV's popular Spring Break show. They performed poolside at the Palms Pool concert in front of legions of swimwear-clad fans who stormed the stage after their performance.

Looking cool before the madness began

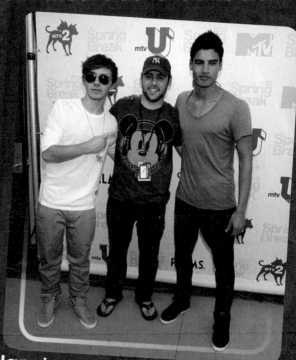

Hanging out with Scooter Braun the industry legend.

The band also popped up at the city's MGM Grand hotel for the 2012 Billboard Music Awards, where they performed 'Glad You Came' and 'Chasing the Sun'

## Blackpool Tower Festival

The guys went down a storm in Blackpool, when they performed as part of the brand spanking new Blackpool Tower Festival. The quintet co-headlined alongside another of Britain's fave boy bands – McFly. They were also able to show new kids on the block, Lawson, how it's done!

## T4 on the Beach

The lads were ecstatic when they signed up for this year's T4OTB. As well as performing, they guest presented, interviewed other acts and, in the name of 'viewer's entertainment', went on some quite scary fairground rides.

## Perez Hilton

The Wanted appeared at celeb blogger Perez's One Night in London bash, with Jedward!

## Capital FM

The lads were on the bill at the station's star-studded Summertime Ball

# THE BIG WA

1. The youngest member of The Wanted is Tom.

**TRUE OR FALSE**

☐     ☐

2. Jay is from Bolton

**TRUE OR FALSE**

☐     ☐

3. Max used to play football for England Schoolboys.

**TRUE OR FALSE**

☐     ☐

4. The single 'Glad You Came' has sold over 3 million copies in the US.

**TRUE OR FALSE**

☐     ☐

5. Siva's star sign is Scorpio.

**TRUE OR FALSE**

☐     ☐

...OR FALSE

**6. The band's debut single was called 'Heart Vacancy'**

TRUE OR FALSE

☐ ☐

**7. Nathan's middle name is James.**

TRUE OR FALSE

☐ ☐

**8. Jay's favourite food is spaghetti Bolognese**

TRUE OR FALSE

☐ ☐

**9. Tom's greatest fear is enclosed spaces.**

TRUE OR FALSE

☐ ☐

**10. The Wanted formed in 2007.**

TRUE OR FALSE

☐ ☐

# THE WANTED WORDSEARCH

There are a dozen Wanted words hiding in this letter grid - can you find each and every one? Study the rows and columns carefully. The hidden words could be running in any direction, including back-to-front!

| O | Y | T | L | B | L | I | U | R | T | M | F |
|---|---|---|---|---|---|---|---|---|---|---|---|
| T | A | L | M | S | E | C | I | R | M | O | T |
| A | U | D | I | T | I | O | N | E | O | S | D |
| I | A | U | E | M | E | U | T | T | N | D | D |
| L | Y | U | I | I | N | I | B | S | D | R | U |
| S | P | A | C | L | L | A | B | E | S | A | B |
| D | N | N | T | R | L | I | F | H | I | Z | L |
| N | U | B | O | L | T | O | N | C | U | I | I |
| E | I | C | P | L | P | S | N | N | S | L | N |
| I | N | B | E | G | U | I | T | A | R | N | P |
| R | C | N | R | O | U | Q | R | M | I | L | N |
| F | U | E | A | T | A | T | U | O | O | P | T |

BASEBALL     FANMILY     LIZARDS
CAPS     FOOTBALL     MANCHESTER
BOLTON     FRIENDS     PIANO
DUBLIN     GUITAR     QUORN

There is a secret, thirteenth word somewhere in the wordsearch square. Can you find it? It's where the boys from The Wanted began. Write the word in the space below.

_ _ _ _ _ _ _ _

26

# THE BOYS AND THE BIEBZ

Ever since Justin Bieber invited The Wanted to open for him during the South American leg of his My World tour, the guys have developed a close bond. They have a natural affiliation after all, being über-gorgeous pop stars adored by millions of fans. JB and the band also share the same management – Scooter Braun is now steering The Wanted to Stateside success.

When Justin popped over to London to turn on the Christmas lights at Westfield, the boys made sure that they were on hand to greet him. Most recently they have been tweeting their mutual appreciation, with Biebz writing, 'Heard you fools killed it on Leno tonight. Gonna check it out. Well done mates!' Max also tweeted, '@justinbieber loving the new song! Great work little brother! #boyfriend.'

**The lads have loads in common with the Canadian heart throb, too. Can you write the correct band member's name in the slots to complete these facts?**

① ...................................... and Justin Bieber have both won awards for their tweeting prowess.

② ............................................. likes books by Terry Goodkind. JB's YouTube username 'kidrauhl' stems from a character called Lord Rahl in a Goodkind novel. Justin's dad is a Goodkind fan and calls himself 'Lordrauhl', hence JB's tag 'Kidrauhl'.

③ ...................................... and Bieber both love black trainers and hi-tops with white soles.

④ ................................... recently taught Brooklyn Beckham to play 'Wonderwall' by Oasis on the guitar, during the soundcheck before a Wanted gig in LA. Justin has also been hanging with the Beckham boys and recently presented Brooklyn, Romeo and Cruz with guitars that he'd signed for them.

⑤ ................................... and Biebz both grew up listening to the music of Boyz II Men, citing them as a major musical influence in their lives.

⑥ ............., ............... and .................... share a love of reptiles with Justin, who has a small boa-constrictor called Johnson, which he once brought to an awards show as his 'plus one!' Eek!

# WANT THAT

Has there ever been a more stylish boy band?
Most groups have struggled through an early cringeworthy 'sack the stylist' period, but our boys seem to have emerged unscathed in the style stakes with a savvy mix of smart tailored pieces and edgy casual wear. Let's sneak a peek inside The Wanted wardrobe.

This season Nathan will be mostly wearing…
## BASEBALL CAPS

The star loves to wear his cap with anything, whether its at an angle, backwards or pulled down low for when he's feeling sheepish or tired. Max calls Nathan's enduring love for this item of headgear 'an obsession'.

Max will be mostly wearing…
## VESTS

No, not as underwear to stop him from getting chilly, as outer wear worn with confidence! The boy is a paid up member of Vest Wearers UK and he subscribes to Vests Monthly Magazine*.

*OK, we made that up, but he does love a vest and with guns like that, who can blame him?

Tom will be mostly wearing…
## T-SHIRTS WITH KERAZY SLOGANS!

Tom just loves to make a statement. He's been emblazoned with prints of his fave soft drink to wordy slogans such as 'Work less, party more, sleep on the bus'!

# WARDROBE!

Jay will be mostly wearing…

## SHIRTS

Possibly checked, often over a loose Tee and sometimes, as in the 2012 calendar, with a floral Hawaiian print accessorized with beaded bracelets and a furry monkey. Well, why not?

Siva will be mostly wearing…

## JACKETS

In all types. The former model knows how to work them in every shape and form – from tailored styles to add a formal touch to fitted leather or in colder weather a wool pea coat, Siva rocks the lot.

## THE WANTED'S FASHION DO'S AND DON'TS

 WANTED IN THE WARDROBE

HOODIES
LEATHER BIKER JACKETS
LUMBERJACK SHIRTS
JEANS
T-SHIRTS
TAILORED SUITS

 WANTED IN THE CHARITY BAG

CUTE AND KOOKY
DICKIE BOW TIES
CRAVATS
SOCKS AND SANDALS
REAL FUR
DAY-GLO ANIMAL PRINT
TROUSERS ALA LMFAO

# WHO SAID THAT?

The Wanted boys love to chat, but how well have you been listening? Read the speech bubbles and then write the correct band members name under each quote.

"I watched Ghost in the West End. Hilarious! But I did sob a bit at the end."

1 .....................

"My first kiss was awful. I leaned in for a kiss on a summer's evening and I bit her lip and she was actually bleeding... but I learnt my lesson – never to kiss too hard."

2 .....................

"You won't find us sitting on stools in suits and standing up for the key change!"

3 .....................

"Am I the most masculine member? Maybe! But actually, out of all the boys, I'm the most affectionate"

5 .....................

"My whole family are football nutters – I wasn't at all. I was a little fat kid who watched TV."

4 .....................

"We've taught the Saturdays how to play football, but they haven't taught us anything."

6 ..........................

"There aren't enough Irish boy bands now – there's just me, and Niall from 1D – oh, and Jedward."

7 ..........................

"We aim to write some mediocre songs then eventually some of them turn out quite good... I'm kidding!"

8 ..........................

"We are just normal guys, who have grown up in normal places and all of this stuff is happening to us."

9 ..........................

"Girls do pretend they find us attractive now we're famous. Before our number one I couldn't pull a bird for the life of me."

10 ..........................

"We make ridiculous comments in interviews most of the time, and we thought we'd have to change ourselves a little bit and become more media trained, but surprisingly the Americans like a bit of rough."

11 ..........................

# DISCOGRAPHY

The Wanted have been rocking the charts ever since they burst onto the music scene three years ago. The guys have already gifted us with two incredible albums and seven amazing singles! Over the pond, the band's first EP release is also making waves. From the string-laden ballad 'Heart Vacancy' to the anthemic club feel of 'Glad You Came', the hits just keep on coming.

## ALBUMS

### THE WANTED
Released: 25th October 2010

### BATTLEGROUND
Released: 4th November 2011

## SINGLES

### ALL TIME LOW
Released: 25th July 2010

### HEART VACANCY
Released 17th October 2010

### LOSE MY MIND
Released: 26th December 2010

### GOLD FOREVER (FOR COMIC RELIEF)
Released 13th March 2011

### GLAD YOU CAME
Released: 10th July 2011

### LIGHTNING
Released: 16th October 2011

### WARZONE
Released: 26th December 2011

### CHASING THE SUN
Released: 20th May 2012

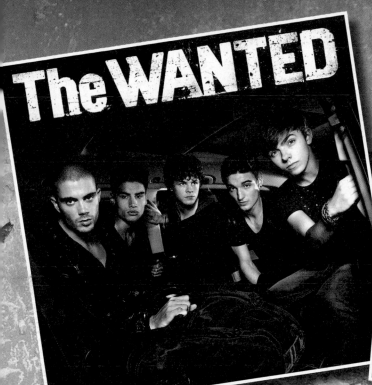

The WANTED

The WANTED
BATTLEGROUND

WANTED
ALL TIME LOW

The WANTED
HEART VACANCY

The WANTED
GOLD FOREVER

RED NOSE DAY

WANTED

The WANTED
LIGHTNING

The WANTED
CHASING THE SUN

# ON CAMERA

## Music Videos

The lads love shooting the music videos for their songs. Sure, there's a lot of waiting around involved, but they also get to fly out to exotic locations like Ibiza, New York and L.A. where they find themselves being filmed at cool pool-parties, banging, hill-top raves or, er.standing on top of piles of rubble…

Here's how things went down on set.

## Glad You Came

The video for 'Glad You Came' was created by Julien Christian Lutz, aka Director X. It was shot on and around the island of Ibiza on two cameras with an international crew. Jay said of the concept, "The theory of the video was to take The Wanted to Ibiza and just film everything and then cut bits that were useable. But the girls were models, they weren't just girls we picked." The party feel of the footage combined with the track itself became the soundtrack to Summer 2011, and in turn the band's most successful release to date. Scenes included the lads watching a stunning sunset, attending a banging club night, having fun on the beach, hanging on a cool yacht and holding a wild party at a villa. Wish we were there!

# Lightning

The music video for 'Lightning' was directed by Matt Stawsi. For this single, the group flew out to a ranch in the Hollywood Hills. Nathan joked, "I don't know why we couldn't have filmed it in the UK in a forest or something, but then we got a free holiday out of it. Can't complain." While waiting for the sun to set Jay and Max amused themselves by doing impressions of plants trying to grow in the arid landscape with soil as dry as ash. Max was hobbling slightly as the day before he'd picked a wasp out of the pool to save it from drowning, then accidentally trodden on it and got himself stung.

When night fell the shoot began and the lads were joined on-set by legions of extras clad in bikinis and shorts. The theme of the song called for lots of explosions provided by the pyrotechnics expert who had worked on several Quentin Tarantino movies. It was a long night that didn't wrap until 6am. By the end the guys had gone slightly crazy with exhaustion, with Siva learning salsa steps from some Brazilian extras and Nathan, Tom and Max in hysterics because the BMX tricksters they'd hired especially turned out not to be able to do any jumps or stunts. As Nathan said, "that's not BMX-ing, that's just riding a bike!"

# Warzone

Director X was back behind the camera for 'Warzone', shooting the clip on a super hi-tech Red digital camera in New York. The boys performed the break-up song in the midst of a war-torn landscape with explosions happening all around them. They had to be on their guard as there was a lot of fire – Nathan – who was on a low that day as Man U were being slaughtered by Man City at football – was filmed playing a flaming piano on a scrapheap, while Jay and Siva had to stand on a burning car. Between takes the boys kept warm with heated hand pouches with cheeky Max stashing his down his trousers for an extra blast of warmth! The final shots showed all five boys returning home to find their girls cheating on them. Now we're really heading into the realms of fantasy!

# ON CAMERA

## Chasing The Sun

'Co-written and produced by UK Rapper Example and was chosen as the title single for the brilliant animated film Ice Age 4: Continental Drift. The Wanted's amazing single 'Chasing The Sun' was a summer anthem and reached number 2 in the UK chart carrying on the boy's chart success!

The first video for 'Chasing The Sun' was released in April 2012. The video was set around the Rosslyn Hotel and the Los Angeles area in the middle of the night. It begins with each of the boys in various clubs and situations meeting different women. When the mysterious women touch each boy they suddenly appear with the same tattoos!

The video follows the boys through their different scenarios and ends on the roof of the Rosslyn Hotel at sunrise. The women they are with turn out to be vampires and bite each of the boys. The closing scene is a group shot of the boys leaving the club into the bright sun. The video has been a massive success with over 14million hits on YouTube.

The second video for 'Chasing The Sun' was made specifically for the film Ice Age 4: Continental Drift and was also the closing title for the film. The film was released in June and July and became a box office smash around the world! The video features the boys performing on blocks of ice in the Arctic Ocean.

The boys are seen having fun and performing alongside characters from the film such as Manny, Sid and Diego and also featured in various clips from the film. The video ends with the sun setting behind a mountain.

# AND THE AWA

The Wanted trophy cabinet is already groaning under the weight of the gongs that they've brought back home! As more and more nominations pour in, the lads are amassing quite a collection of statuettes, plates, discs and oddly-shaped crystal.
Check out some of the highlights so far...

# ...RD GOES TO...

## 4MUSIC AWARDS 2010

| | |
|---|---|
| Hottest Boys | Won |
| Biggest Breakthrough | Won |
| Best Video – 'All Time Low' | Nominated |

## VIRGIN MEDIA MUSIC AWARDS 2010

| | |
|---|---|
| Best Newcomer | Won |
| Best Group | Won |

## ARQIVA AWARDS 2011

| | |
|---|---|
| Best UK Breakthrough Artist | Won |

## BRIT AWARDS 2011

| | |
|---|---|
| Best British Single – All Time Low | Nominated |

## BBC RADIO 1 TEEN AWARDS 2011

| | |
|---|---|
| Best British Music Act | Won |

## BRIT AWARDS 2012

| | |
|---|---|
| Best British Single 'Glad You Came' | Nominated |

## Did you know?

...in 2011 two of the band's members won personal commendations.

Try and name the winner of each of the plaudits below.

Celebritain.com
Best Celebrity Tweeter

Won by

PETA UK
Sexiest Celebrity Vegetarian

Won by

# LADS ON TOUR

Never mind their success across the pond, just look at what The Wanted continue to accomplish on home turf! In the space of just three short years, the boys have graduated from performing in school halls and pubs, to selling out the nation's top arenas. They've now played to packed venues in every corner of their homeland. Check out The Wanted's packed tour schedule.

## THE CODE ARENA TOUR 2012

| 15/02 | Capital FM Arena | Nottingham |
| 17/02 | MEN Arena | Manchester |
| 18/02 | Motorpoint Arena | Sheffield |
| 20/02 | The Brighton Centre | Brighton |
| 23/02 | Motorpoint Arena | Cardiff |
| 24/02 | Echo Arena | Liverpool |
| 25/02 | Metro Radio Arena | Newcastle |
| 27/02 | S.E.C.C | Glasgow |
| 28/02 | A.E.C.C | Aberdeen |
| 01/03 | LG Arena | Birmingham |
| 02/03 | International Centre | Bournemouth |
| 03/03 | The 02 Arena | London |
| 05/03 | The Brighton Centre | Brighton |
| 06/03 | International Centre | Bournemouth |
| 08/03 | Odyssey Arena | Belfast |
| 09/03 | The 02 | Dublin |

# EXTRA GIGS

The guys' performances extended way past the initial official dates when the racing and festival seasons kicked in.
In June 2012, at Crocke Park in Dublin, The Wanted gave an excellent performance which raised the excitement before Westlife came on to the stage to perform their last ever Gig.
Other Gigs included T in the Park, Summertime Ball, Olympic Torch Relay Celebrations in Birmingham & Hyde Park and T4 On The Beach.

# TOUR SCRAPBOOK

## MEN ARENA MANCHESTER

## MAX'S MANOR

The Manchester gig was always going to be a special one for Mancunian Max. Months beforehand he was waxing lyrical about how the experience would feel. He told the Manchester Evening News "I can't believe we'll be playing the M.E.N Arena – that's the one venue more than any in the world that I've wanted to perform in, so that really is going to be a bit special for me." And on the night he was feeling just as excited. Interviewed backstage by Rob Ellis from Capital Breakfast, the boys joked that the gig was sold out because Max's friends and family had bought all the tickets. There were certainly a lot of George's and Max-mates in the house, as he admitted he had booked 80 seats so all his peeps could come and see the band in action. Awww!

## LIVERPOOL LOVES 'YA

'Liverpool? Are you having a good night?' Max yelled to the packed crowd in the city's iconic Echo Arena. And the Liverpuddlians certainly seemed to be enjoying themselves. The crowd went wild for Siva, Max, Nathan, Tom and Jay, lapping up every song from the thumping 'Lightning' to the almost melancholic 'Gold Forever'. The lads, looking slick in black, with the odd pop of colour such as Nathan's dapper red blazer - seemed in a particularly playful mood, bouncing around the set with Jay conducting the adoring audience in a game of cheers and boos. 'Glad You Came?' You betcha!

# TOUR SCRAPBOOK

## SECC GLASGOW

### OCH AY GUYS!

Their last Glasgow tour date was at the Clyde Auditorium, but this time The Wanted were back in the city on a much bigger and noisier scale, with huge pyrotechnics and better harmonies. Max explained that Warzone 'is a song about a girl cheating on a guy' and dedicated it to the lads in the crowd – but he could barely be heard above the girls' devoted screams.

At this gig the fans' screams almost lifted the roof from the LG Arena.
The welcome was particularly warm because the Midlands is Nathan's old stomping ground. The Gloucester-born boy told the crowd; "It's so good to be here, at my local arena." So throughout the gig Nathan's solos and – as he puts it – 'warbly bits' were received with huge cheers, as was the cool Coldplay medley and their newest tracks. The boys once more showcased their considerable musical talents, playing instruments and delivering pitch-perfect vocals.

# TOUR SCRAPBOOK

## 02 ARENA LONDON

## WELCOME HOME

After taking the USA by storm you might have thought the return to British soil would be a comedown for the lads, but no. They were back in style and kicked off their sell-out arena tour with a sizzling opening night at London's massive O2 Arena. Bursting onto the stage in plumes of smoke, the lads, clad in black flack jackets and combat trousers, looked like the sexiest SAS soldiers ever recruited. The air was filled with screams as they worked through their catalogue of hits, surprised everyone with a medley of Coldplay hits and then got the entire crowd on their feet with 'Glad You Came'.

# LAST NIGHT

They started the 'The Code' tour at the O2 in London, so what better final venue than The O2 in Dublin. It was a particularly special night for the gorgeous Siva, who tweeted before the gig; "... HOME!!!!!! :D ready to perform #TheCode at the O2 Dublin tonight!!!!!!". The proud Dubliner ended the gig wrapped in an Irish flag and beaming from ear to ear.

# Get Arty

The group's CD covers to date have all featured the boys themselves, but The Wanted also love freestyle art. Jay, in particular, is an avid doodler! Think about the band's next album – can you imagine what title and design the group might go for? Use the opposite page to create some eye-popping new artwork to wow the fans.

# FRONT ALBUM COVER

## BACK ALBUM COVER

Stuck for inspiration?

Pick the album name first and then let that set the tone for the art style.

If you want to show the guys themselves, try sketching caricatures or creating a funny cartoon.

Find people hard to draw? Why not go for bold graphics or a unique abstract design.

Think about The Wanted's style, their ethos and what makes them tick. Try and create an album cover that matches the look and feel of the graphics you've seen in their concert programmes, stage costumes or their website.

Don't forget to add a track list on the back. Think up the titles you'd like the band to sing!

# WHO'S YOUR MOST WANTED?

Which of the Wanted guys is your true soul-mate? Max, Siva, Jay, Tom and Nathan are all so gorgeous, it can be hard to choose between them. This test will give you a helping hand – answer the quiz questions then check the verdict at the back of the book.

## 1. YOU BUY SOMETHING NEW FOR YOUR BEDROOM. IS IT

a. a new flatscreen TV?
b. a cool new cage for your pet hamster?
c. a big mirror?
d. some scented candles and a new duvet?
e. a new stereo with huge speakers?

## 2. YOU'RE OUT SHOPPING AND FANCY A SNACK. DO YOU

a. grab a bacon buttie?
b. pick some Quorn savoury eggs or a piece of fruit?
c. have a bowl of soup?
d. choose a chocolate brownie – you just can't resist!
e. find a fast food joint?

## 3. AT SCHOOL YOU'RE KNOWN AS BEING

a. sporty but naughty.
b. clever and articulate.
c. outgoing and popular.
d. cute but shy.
e. a joker who can be focussed when you're into something.

## 4. AT THE SCHOOL PROM OR DISCO YOU'LL BE THE ONE WHO

a. pranks the teachers.
b. slips over and spills drink over yourself.
c. has girls queuing up to dance with you.
d. is crowned prom queen.
e. Plays a set with your band or takes a turn as DJ.

## 5. YOUR FAVOURITE WAY TO SPEND A SATURDAY AFTERNOON IS

a. playing or watching sport.
b. horse riding or walking your dog.
c. going clothes shopping then taking a trip to the cinema.
d. chilling with your family or friends.
e. hanging with your mates and listening to music.

## 6. A CUTE GIRL OR BOY MOVES IN NEXT DOOR. THE THING ABOUT HIM THAT CATCHES YOUR EYE IS HIS

a. brooding stare and gorgeous pout.
b. sense of humour and unruly mop of hair.
c. gorgeous smile and sparkling white teeth.
d. cheekbones and glossy black hair.
e. twinkly eyes and long dark lashes.

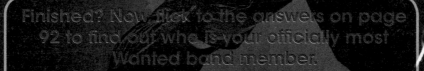

Finished? Now flick to the answers on page 92 to find out who is your officially most Wanted band member.

# WHAT'S IN A NAME?

Do The Wanted boys suit their names? Read the summaries below, then see if you can decide which name is being described each time. Now fill in the correct letter to match the monikers to the correct owners.

**A** Currently ranked the sixth most popular boy's name in the UK by the Office for National Statistics, this name is frequently abbreviated. It comes from the Greek form of the Aramaic name (Ta'oma') which means 'twin'.

**B** This moniker is of Roman origin and means 'the greatest'. It is very popular in Germany, England, Scandinavia and the Netherlands. In England it's twenty-third on the table of most common boys' names.

**C** This noble name, which means 'he who supplants', stems from the Latin Iacomus. It's been in use in England since the 13th century and has been given to several English and Scottish kings. The name has also been borne by no less than six American presidents!

**D** Derived from the Hebrew, this name means 'he gave'. In the Bible's Old Testament, it also refers to a prophet. Others might recognise it as the male lead character with the surname 'Detroit' in the musical Guys And Dolls.

**E** This exotic name is said to be derived from that of an important Hindu God. It is also the title of a Sri Lankan Tamil film which was released in 1989 and is a famous hero's name in South Indian movie culture.

# THE BIG WANTED QUIZ
## PICK THE PICTURE

Seconds out, it's round two of the massive Wanted quiz! This time you'll need to have sharp eyes and ahead for triv. Read all ten of the statements and then draw a line to the correct band member that is being referred to each time. Can you score a perfect ten?

1. I am a skilled tap dancer.

2. I am one of eight siblings.

3. I am a huge fan of Boyz II Men.

4. My nickname is Roy.

5. My star sign is Virgo.

6. I love candles.

7. I am a dedicated Manchester United fan.

8. My favourite animal is the Great White Shark.

9. I love the music of Oasis.

10. I have an identical twin called Thomas.

# FESTIVAL FEVER

Tunes by The Wanted are played in clubs and at parties every summer, so it's no wonder that the band are such a hit on the festival circuit. In 2011 they played to huge crowds at V, the iTunes festival and T4 Party on the Beach. By the next year they were everywhere – from T in The Park, to the Blackpool Tower Festival and Hyde Park's Torch Relay Concert.

## DID YOU KNOW THAT AT V...

- Tom was desperate to stay and watch the Manic Street Preachers and Pendulum.
- Siva engaged in his usual pre-show ritual of untying and retying the laces on his right trainer.

## DID YOU KNOW THAT AT ITUNES...

- The boys played ping pong backstage while waiting to perform and Max and Tom had a heated debate about the score line. Max won.
- Tom admitted to being a massive Foo Fighters fan.
- Max said that he thought Siva would beat him into having babies.
- Siva admitted that the pots of moisturiser on their rider were for him.

## DID YOU KNOW THAT AT T4 PARTY ON THE BEACH...

- The boys divulged their best and worst beach memories. Tom's best recollection was riding donkeys on Blackpool beach, while poor Siva's worst one was of being dug into the sand by his brothers who then left him half-buried.
- Jay and Max had a backstage dance-off, resulting in victory for... Jay! Tom admitted he's the worst of the bunch, although he can perform one breakdance move – the caterpillar.

# COMMON GROUND

When you're together 24/7, it helps if you have stuff in common. Here are just a few of the things that bind The Wanted's members together not just as band-mates, but as friends too.

Both Jay and Siva have twin brothers. Jay's is called Thomas and Siva's is named Kumar.

Tom and Max both enjoy weight training, often lifting weights in their dressing rooms.

Jay and Nathan both had their eyes on a career on the stage, attending drama schools. Jay attended the Midlands Academy of Dance and Drama (MADD) while Nathan went to Sylvia Young.

Max and Jay own lizards as pets and love the outdoors. Jay's favourite programmes are nature documentaries while Max recently expressed a desire to appear on a Bear Grylls Wild Weekends episode.

Nathan and Max both share a love of footie, although their teams (Man City and Man United) are rivals.

Tom and Max both auditioned for the X Factor. Tom didn't make it through the heats,

Siva and Nathan are both self-confessed country boys who love the charms of the countryside, while Jay, Max and Tom prefer city life.

Tom and Jay share the same star sign – Leo, while the pair and Nathan are all Fire signs. No wonder they're bezzies!

Max and Siva both cite Michael Jackson as a major musical influence.

Nathan and Max love the movie The Lion King.

# IT'S A TW BROMANCE

They're no doubt that The Wanted lads love each other to bits! Fill in the blanks to reveal who's said what about who.

**1. NATHAN ON** _____

"LIKES SILK BED SHEETS, SCENTED CANDLES WEIRD BEHAVIOUR TO BE EXPECTED BUT IT'S ALL A PART OF HIM BEING ONE OF THE NICEST PEOPLE YOU COULD EVER MEET.

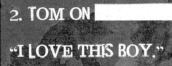

**2. TOM ON** _____

"I LOVE THIS BOY."

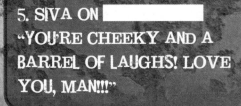

**3. MAX ON** _____

"HE IS A LOVELY YOUNG MAN, FULL OF TALENT AND HAPPINESS."

**4. JAY ON** _____

"NOT A BAD BONE IN HIS BODY. I WANT TO MARRY HIS SOUL."

**5. SIVA ON** _____

"YOU'RE CHEEKY AND A BARREL OF LAUGHS! LOVE YOU, MAN!!!"

# BUCKING T

You might have guessed by now that The Wanted are not your average boy band. The guys have managed to take pop's rule book and twisted it on its head! Wanna know what they've done to buck the boy band trend? Put your tongue firmly in your cheek and read on...

## THE WANTED MANTRA V THE BOYBAND MANTRA

| THE WANTED MANTRA | THE BOYBAND MANTRA |
|---|---|
| We sometimes wear matching clothes, we will definitely look back in the future and say, "why didn't I listen to the stylist?" | We will always wear matching clothes. |
| We rehearse simple choreography over and over and then usually scrap it and jump on the spot like a kid that needs the toilet. | We will always pull off seamless choreography with apparent ease and massive grins. |
| We have girlfriends sometimes, famous or non-famous. | We will be single. |
| Tom will be topless when the climate would indicate he should prefer to be clothed. The rest of us will dress as the temperature dictates. | We will be topless, when the climate would indicate we would prefer to be clothed. |
| We only lip-sync when the TV studio does not use live vocals and we will suck at it. If however, you come and see us live, our vocal chords, lungs, diaphragms and teeth will work to create real sounds you will actually hear. | We will get really, really, good at lip-synching. |

# THE TREND

| | |
|---|---|
| We have neat hair when we are somewhere that requires neat hair and bed heads the rest of the time – and not cool bed heads either, rank ones. Except Max. | We will have fashionable, asymmetrical hair styles. |
| We have bodies ranging from muscly to skinny, tall to small, depending on what our DNA says. | We will have bodies that would make the Chippendales jealous. |
| We have regular meetings with our record company because we spoke utter rubbish during an interview – often forgetting to mention the reason why we were being interviewed. | We will execute perfectly rehearsed interview answers. |
| We approach a key change with extreme caution. It's a powerful weapon not to be used lightly… | We will demand a key change. |
| We rely on each other, we go on holiday together. It's fun. We will continue to give you everything we can, on and off stage, because you… the TWFanmily have given us everything we have. | We will tolerate each other while the money's good. |

63

# WANTED!!

The Wanted don't have the manufactured, squeaky clean image so often cultivated by other boy bands in the past, which makes us love them all the more. In the US, the guys are even known as 'the bad boys from England'!

Think about Max, Siva, Jay, Tom and Nathan. Who has the naughtiest glint in their eye? Find some pencils or felt-tips, then sketch your fave member of the band into this retro Wanted poster.

# IN ANOTHER LIFE

A world without The Wanted is inconceivable, but what would have happened had Max decided to go to the park for a kick about on that fateful audition day? Now imagine if Seev had been visiting family in Ireland or Tom had overslept. What then? Where would their lives have taken them? It's true to say that all of the band members have hidden talents. Think about the jobs they might each have pursued, then write down the names of the ones that best suit their skills and talents.

## 1. Professional footballer

...................................................................

## 2. Top Model

...................................................................

## 3. Top Dancer

...................................................................

## 4. Bin Man

...................................................................

## 5. Member of a Take That tribute Act

...................................................................

## 6. Talent Show Judge

..........................................

## 7. Radio DJ

..........................................

## 8. Tree Surgeon

..........................................

## 9. Animal Rights Campaigner

..........................................

## 10. Wheeler dealer in the family business

..........................................

# BREAKING THE

**Wanted in America? They definitely are! In 2012 the group pulled off the ultimate coup and cracked the notoriously difficult US market. Here's how it happened…**

GRAMERCY THEATRE — THE WANTED SOLD OUT TONIGHT

## THE GRAMERCY THEATRE

On the 25th October 2011 the boys played their first gig stateside. It was a sell out and had fans queuing all the way around the block. The boys absolutely smashed it was their first US gig on the 25 October 2011. The crowd went crazy to Glad You Came which little did they know was about to explode over there.'

## THE ELLEN SHOW

On 10th of January 2012 The Wanted made their US TV debut on *The Ellen DeGeneres Show*. The lads performed a rendition of 'Glad You Came', taking over the set to serenade the audience. The boys received a brilliant reception from the crowd and Ellen joined them on stage to ask where they got their reputation as 'the bad boys of England'. Max replied, 'I think it's to do with the fact we like to party and I think with America and there being so many beautiful women about – we're going to have a good time." The appearance went so well the band later tweeted, 'So pleased you all love our @The Ellen Show performance! Love u all'.

## TV-TASTIC

When they were invited on the popular chat show Tonight With *Jay Leno*, the boys were surprised to see fans storm the stage. Afterwards the guys tweeted, '*Got word that we're the first group ever to have fans rush the stage in @JayLenoTonight history.*' The following day the group appeared on *The View*, before dazzling millions with an amazing appearance on *American Idol*.

# STATES

## THE US TOUR

On the 17th of January 2012, the boys began a ten date tour of the States and Canada, starting in Florida. Many of the dates were sold out with venues being mobbed by crowds of screaming fans . The guys later tweeted their thanks and appreciation to their 'TWUSAFanmily'.

The tour was sold out and with such high demand in LA they had to do a last minute venue change from the Roxy to the El Ray to accommodate the ever growing TWFanmily.

## 'GLAD YOU CAME'

After the boys' unforgettable anthem reached the number 1 spot in the UK in the summer of 2011, the single was released in the US. Their debut performance on the Ellen show shot it straight up the charts where it peaked at number 3 becoming the highest chart position for a British boy band ever. The tune even beat the existing record of number 7 set by Take That's 'Back for Good'. 'Glad you came' has now had over 3million sales in the US

## MTV SPRING BREAK

On 22nd March, 2012, The Wanted appeared on MTV's Spring Break at the Palms Casino Resort in Las Vegas. The lads performed poolside in front of an audience full of bikini-clad girls and seemed to be loving every minute of it. In fact, things got so crazy that the gig had to be shut down for nearly half an hour after a mass stage invasion by fans. The band later tweeted, *Hands down one of the most unreal experiences in our lives. #MTVSpringBreak2012 we will never forget it.'*

## THE EP

On April 24th The Wanted released a ten track EP via Def Jam Records. The disk featured 'All Time Low', 'Lose My Mind' and 'Heart Vacancy' from the first album and 'Gold Forever', 'Lightning', 'Glad You Came' and 'Warzone' from the second, but there were also two brand new tracks including 'Chasing The Sun' penned by British rapper Example. "As soon as someone mentioned The Wanted, I thought it was right. It's all about how they go after the sunshine and the message is partying and fun, free living, let's be young forever." Example (taken from Capital online)

## CAST OF *GLEE* PERFORM 'GLAD YOU CAME'

When The Wanted arrived back in the UK for their The Code tour, it was announced that the cast of *Glee* would perform 'Glad You Came' in an episode of the hit series. The group couldn't believe that things were happening so fast for them in the US. Jay said, "Glee is just as big in the UK, so when we heard we were just like, 'What's going on boys?'" The episode, called On My Way aired on Fox on 21st February. Afterwards the band tweeted, *'Big thanks to @gleeonfox for featuring #GLADYOUCAME & a huge thanks to all our fans for supporting us and getting #TheWantedOnGlee to trend.'*

# MISSING LYRICS
# 'CHASING THE SUN'

You hear it on the radio, hum it in the shower, but how well do you know the band's massive track 'Chasing the Sun'? Read through the lines of lyrics, then try and fill in the blanks just from memory – no cheating! Now flick to answers on page 92 to see how accurate you were.

I'm better, so much . . . . . . now
I see the lights touch the light?
Were . . . . . . . . now
I'm better, so much better now
. . . . to the skys
Give me live
Were together now

We've only just begun
. . . . . . . . . . . by drums
Until forever comes
You'll find us . . . . . . . . the sun

They said this day . . . . . . . . come
We refused to run
We've only . . . . . begun
You'll find us chasing the sun

Oh oh oh oh oh oh
Oh oh oh oh oh oh
Oh oh oh oh oh oh
You'll . . . . us chasing the sun

Oh oh oh oh oh oh
Oh oh oh oh oh oh
Oh oh oh oh oh oh
You'll find us chasing the . . . .

When the daylight's . . . . . .
We're gonna play in the dark
Till it's golden . . . . .
And now it feels so . . . . . . . .
Can see you coming
. . . . we'll never grow old again
You'll find us chasing the sun

I'm never, I'm never . . . . .
Lying here staring up
And you're . . . . . . . down
I'm never, I'm never down
. . . . . forever, forever
With you around

We've only just . . . . .
Hypnotized by drums
Until forever . . . . . .
You'll find us chasing the sun

70

They said this day . . . . . . . come
We . . . . . . . to run
We've only just begun
You'll find us chasing the sun
The sun, The sun, The sun, The sun, The
sun, The sun, The . . . ,
You'll find us chasing the sun

Oh oh oh oh oh oh
Oh oh oh oh oh oh
Oh oh oh oh oh oh
You'll find us . . . . . . the sun

Oh oh oh oh oh oh
Oh oh oh oh oh oh
Oh oh oh oh oh oh
You'll . . . . . us chasing the sun

When the . . . . . . . fading
We're gonna play in the dark
Till it's . . . . . . . again
And now it feels so amazing
Can see you coming
And we'll never grow . . . . again
You'll find us chasing the sun

Ohhh ohhh ohhh, Chasing the sun
Ohhh ohhhohhhohhh, Chasing the sun
Ohhh ohhh ohhh, You'll find us
Chasing the sun
Ohhh ohhhohhhohhh , You'll find us
chasing the sun

When the daylight's fading
We're gonna play in the . . . .
Till it's golden again
And . . . . it feels so amazing
Can see you coming
And we'll . . . . . . grow old again

You'll find us chasing the sun

Oh oh oh oh oh oh
Oh oh oh oh oh oh
Oh oh oh oh oh oh
You'll . . . . . us chasing the sun

Oh oh oh oh oh oh
Oh oh oh oh oh oh
Oh oh oh oh oh oh
You'll find us chasing the sun

# THE BIG WANTE
## ROUND 3
## TRICKY TRIVIA

OK clever clogs, here's a tick test to get your rummaging in your Wanted archives! Stage three of this testing TW quiz is crammed with triv, deets and lesser known facts about the fab five. How quickly can you complete all ten?

Which Pop-Star invited The Wanted on their South American Tour?

a. Lady Gaga. ☐

b. Justin Bieber. ☐

c. Jessie J. ☐

2. What does Max's gran call trousers?

a. Strides. ☐

b. Kecks. ☐

c. Pull ups. ☐

3. Which member of the group has a pet snake called Charlie?

a. Max. ☐

b. Jay. ☐

c. Nathan. ☐

4. Which programme did Max recently tweet that he'd like to go on?

a. Bear Grylls: Wild Weekends. ☐

b. Coronation Street. ☐

c. Match of the Day. ☐

5. Which members of the band are one of twins?

a. Siva and Max. ☐

b. Siva and Jay. ☐

c. Siva and Tom. ☐

6. Which one of these TV shows was Jay's fave childhood viewing?

a. You've Been Framed. ☐

b. Xena Warrior Princess. ☐

c. Postman Pat. ☐

# QUIZ

7. Which member of Take That did Tom most often impersonate in his band Take That II?

a. Gary Barlow. ☐

b. Jason Orange. ☐

c. Mark Owen. ☐

8. Which of the guys once had an embarrassing moment when his trousers fell down at the Arqiva Awards?

a. Siva. ☐

b. Tom. ☐

c. Jay. ☐

9. Which of these places have the boys from The Wanted not visited to film a video?

a. Coney Island, New York. ☐

b. Oahu, Hawaii. ☐

c. Ibiza. ☐

10. Which of these has not been a holiday destination for the lads?

a. Brazil. ☐

b. Benidorm. ☐

c. Barbados. ☐

# WANTED BY NUM8ER5

**3**

The number on the US Billboard 100 chart that 'Glad You Came' reached.

**16.99**

The bargain price of an official The Wanted doll.

**23**

The total number of dates the band played during the Behind Bars and The Code Tours.

**43**

The number of weeks their debut single 'All Time Low' spent in the UK charts.

**287**

The total number of weeks The Wanted have spent in the UK charts.
(according to the Official Charts Company).

**15,000**

The number of revellers who packed the Blue Tent at the V Festival to watch the guys perform.

**473,158** AND COUNTING

The Mammoth sales of the 'The Wanted' album.

**2,100,000** AND COUNTING

The number of likes on the wanted Facebook Page.

**3,570,140** AND COUNTING

The number of combind followers for the wantted Twitter account.
@thewantedmusic @SivaTheWanted @NathanTheWanted @MaxTheWanted @TomTheWanted @JayTheWanted

**48,868,656+**

The views for the 'Glad You Came' official vid on YouTube and Vevo.

# MiXed-up MuSic

Unscramble the crazy anagrams below to find ten top tracks from The Wanted's back catalogue.

**GLAUCOMA DYE**

_ _ _ _ _ _ _   _ _ _ _ _

**SLANDERERS POLIO**

_ _ _ _ _ _ _   _ _ _ _ _ _

**BE TROLLEYS HURTING**

_ _ _ _ _ _ _   _ _ _ _ _ _ _ _ _

**A TOWEL MILL**

_ _ _ _   _ _ _ _ _ _

**TRECKO**

_ _ _ _ _ _

**HAD IN OWL**

_ _ _   _ _ _ _ _

**WEED HE KENT**

_ _ _ _ _ _   _ _ _ _

**RAZE NOW**

_ _ _ _ _ _ _

**DAME**

_ _ _ _

**DEMON SLIMY**

_ _ _ _ _ _   _ _ _ _

# CRAZY FANTASTIC

While being mobbed at LAX airport recently, Nathan described the TW fans as "absolutely awesome"! The TWFanmily certainly is one of the most loyal groups of fans in the world. Are you one of the gang? Congratulations – you are the secret ingredient that make The Wanted phenomenon so special.

## STAR-GAZING

The fans would literally give the sun, moon and stars for their idols. Siva says, "Our fans are crazy and so loyal. We have two stars named after us now, they're called The Wanted and we have the co-ordinates so we can look at the stars. It's really cool!"

## STRANGE REQUESTS

The boys are always receiving bizarre requests via Twitter. Some are cute, some are puzzling and some are downright weird! Siva recalls that "I got asked to tweet a picture to show the colour of my toothbrush, which is a bit weird. I've got no idea why somebody wants to see my scruffy little toothbrush."

## THE WANTED RUSH

When things hit Siva Pitch, as they often do during a The Wanted show or PA, things can get a little out of hand. Jay remembers, "We had one moment at Radio 1, there were that many people waiting for us that the ones at the front were getting crushed. We were trying to get people to move back and putting our hands out to say move back, but they were just grabbing our hands! There were little kids at the front, which was scary, as people could have actually got hurt because of us. Luckily no-one did."

## DETECTIVE WORK

The lads are always surprised by the ingenuity of some of the TWFanmily in their quest to follow the band. Jay says, "We used to tell people where we were going but it got to the point where we couldn't do anything because they were all there. Now I've got no idea how they find us. We were saying if you wanted to improve MI5 security services, get our fans on the case as they work everything out, they are amazing."

# WANTED-ISMS

Did you know that the band and their fans share a special language? Here's a guide to some of the most popular terms and phrases coined by the boys. Read up, then start using your favourite Wanted-isms in every conversation.

**SPASTARD!**
Silly word to use as an insult.

**EYA MATE**
[Greeting] Translates to 'Hello, my friend'. Should always be said with a smile.

**FOOT FIVE**
[Verb] Traditional 'High 5' greeting, but performed foot-to-hand or foot-to-foot.

**G** - Derived from the word 'gangsta' It signifies someone streetwise and successful who listens to rap and wears a lot of bling – "I bin rollin' with ma homies. I'm just so G." Can also be employed ironically to mean 'geek'.

**'H'**
When you are so 'G' you become 'H'

**IT'S A TWTHING**
[Phrase] Used to describe something only a TWFanmily member would understand.

**JAYNIUS**
[Noun-Portmanteau] A person, like Jay with silly or even dumb intelligence that is just… pure genius.

**JIVA**
[Noun-Portmanteau] Used to refer to the TWBromance between Jay and Siva – meaning that they are getting on very well. Jiva is the most common of 20 possible TWBromances including 'JAYTHAN' and 'TOMAX'.

**MAXFACTOR**
[Adjective/Compound] The word used to describe a person or action that has a distinct Max-esque quality.

**Nicely**
a) when a situation is really nice, calm and exciting
b) when you're encouraging someone to do something with manners/caution
c) when you're nicely

**Morrrrrnin**
A way of greeting people in the morning in a strong Gloucester accent
Tweople – TW people who follow The Wanted on Twitter. Also known as a group of people within the TWFanmily.

**PULL-UPS**

[Noun] Old school term for trousers used by Max's nana in phrases like "Your pull-ups are nice dear."

**WANTED WEDNESDAY**

[Noun] TW alternative to the standard Wednesday, when The Wanted and the TWFanmily go mental. WW is about jokes, videos, exclusives and a lot of screaming. It's cosmic and totally rad!

**SIVA BELIEVER**

[Noun] An avid supporter of Siva. They believe one day he will take to his throne as King of Ireland and everyone will hold hands and light scented candles and sing along to The Corrs. See also Siva Fever, used to describe the sensation of being completely enamoured with the singer.

**SYKESATION**

[Noun-Portmanteau] Like Siva Fever, this is used to describe the sensation of being in love with Nathan.

**TOMTRUM**

[Noun-Portmanteau] A sudden burst of childlike anger often displayed by Tom in lines such as "don't have a Tomtrum!"

**TWENTY13**

[Noun-Abbreviation-Portmanteau] Symbolises a new year for The Wanted boys, meaning that this year is theirs.

**Tweople**

TW people who follow The Wanted on Twitter. Also known as a group of people within the TWFanmily

**TWFANOFTHEWEEK**

[Noun-Phrase] A title bestowed on one fan per week for their outstanding services, support for the boys or their creativity.

**WANTED WEEK**

[Noun] Once in a while, around the release of a single or album, or sometimes 'just because', there is a Wanted Week. It is Wanted Wednesday repeated over seven days.

# OLYMPICS 2012

## TORCH RELAY

On June 30th, The Wanted were honoured to be invited to act as official torchbearers in the Olympic Torch Relay, thanks to Coca Cola. The boys proudly carried the iconic flame through the streets of Newton in South Staffordshire in front of an enormous crowd of cheering fans. Shortly afterwards Nathan took to Twitter to express his excitement. "Just ran with the Olympic torch!! Such an unbelievable experience! Never been so grateful for an opportunity in my life!! #goodtimes."

# BIRMINGHAM CONCERT

Later that day the lads were the headline act at The 2012 Olympic Torch Relay Concert in Cannon Hill Park. They treated 2000 die-hard fans – who had penned the boys' names on their foreheads and were holding up signs saying everything from We heart The Wanted, to 'I Want Jay's Lizard' their latest hits including 'Chasing the Sun' and 'Glad You Came'.

# HYDE PARK 2012

The Olympic Celebrations continued in earnest for the band, as they took part in a massive gig in London's Hyde Park, to coincide with the Olympic Torch Relay Finale. They took to the stage the day before the opening ceremony, alongside Dizzee Rascal, and cheeky duo Rizzle Kicks.

# sweet tweets

The lads love a good tweet (who doesn't, these days?), taking to their mobiles and laptops to chat about anything and everything. Take a look at some of the band's best Twitter entries, then log on and start following online.

@TomTheWanted: 'Work hard and you achieve.'

@MaxTheWanted: '3 days til American Idol!!! Very excited.'

@JayTheWanted: 'I really appreciate #DownloadWarzone is trending, it's only with fan support that this song will get the recognition it deserves!! BIGLOVE!'

@TomTheWanted: 'All our fans around the world stick together. This is why I respect you all dearly!'

@JayTheWanted: 'I think I fancy my lizard!!!'

@NathanTheWanted: 'I see @TomTheWanted is making friends with the TOWIE lot... I do wonder why can't we have "the only way is Gloucester?" DOITFORTHESHEEP!!'

@SivaTheWanted: 'It's only St Patricks Day! Have a Guinness on me ;) "Slainte".'

@MaxTheWanted: 'Can people stop calling me bald... It really upsetting me... ;) #hmmmmm.'

@SivaTheWanted: 'Need 2 put a wash on in my hotel room (weird) don't even know where 2 start with this magic machine that cleans ur stuff.'

@TomtheWanted: 'Plane food...plain awful!! http://t.co/7g9eTIbM.'

@JayTheWanted: 'So @scooterbraun @nanotissera and the lads just April fooled the c**p out of me – I'm actually in my hotel room shaking from it. No words.'

@MaxTheWanted: 'Over 1million sales in US!! Amazing amazing amazing! Mint a manc should say.'

@SivaTheWanted: 'Good morning!! TWFanmily! Oh god it's early lol. Who wants breakfast? :).'

@MaxTheWanted: 'Bournemouth!!! My ears are ringin!!! OUCH and thanks!! :) x.'

@JayTheWanted: 'Aaaaaaaaaaaaaaaaaaaaaaaaand I'm out of socks. #travellerslife.'

@SivaTheWanted: 'The last night of our tour #thecode in my home city Dublin was incredible! Thank you so much x.'

@NathanTheWanted: 'RT @MaarianaVella @NathanTheWanted ohana means family. Family means never abandon or forget right? #TWFanmily.'

@MaxTheWanted: 'Got football manager and films ready for the flight.... #prepared.'

@TomTheWanted: 'On a bad note. I lost my bank card in the pandemonium! If anyone finds it, can you message me. I will personally meet you #findtomsbankcard.'

@JayTheWanted: 'Took a minute to think what my first tweet this year should say...erm, that's all I got. #TWBoom.'

@MaxTheWanted: 'Congrats to @justinbieber with biggest villain at the NME Awards... Now that's a birthday present!!'

@NathanTheWanted 'Wow soo many english peeps out in LA right now! Might put together a british gathering where we can all sit round a fire drinking tea!'

@SivaTheWanted: 'Everyone who gave me a note today will get a tweet from me. Really appreciate you all for coming x. Amazing!'

## who's bio is it anyway?

Write the name of the band member underneath their official Twitter Bio

Writing. Use factor 50 sunscreen. Avatar. All good

.........................................

In The Wanted, next stop, WORLD

.........................................

Look like a mixture of sid the sloth, stewie griffin and E.T. ...Not on strike...Atm ;)

.........................................

Irish New Single: WARZONE...Check It Out

.........................................

Live, Dream, Don't Exist.

.........................................

# I'M GONNA USE MY MIND

Now it's time to work that grey matter again– see what we did with the title there? Find a pencil and a comfy chair, then see how many words you can make from the statement below. You can only use each letter once. To make this even trickier set yourself a time limit and challenge a friend to a word-off!

## THE WANTED ROCK MY WORLD

85

# THE BIG WANTED QUIZ

## THE ULTIMATE CHALLENGE

Well done, you've reached the final part of the TW quiz. Complete this and you'll really be a 'Jaynius'! This time there's nowhere to hide – no 50/50 guesswork or multiple choice get-out clause. Think hard, write your answer in the space below each question, then turn to the back of the book to mark your answers.

How did the band get 'Punk'd' on the recent TV show of the same name?

Which band member once said they had a soft spot for Lady Gaga?

What is the abbreviation of the dance and drama school that Jay attended?

Which member of TW has the most followers on Twitter?

What in TW terminology are 'pythons?

**Which Disney movie do Nathan and Max both love?**

**What happened when The Wanted appeared on the *Jay Leno Show* and at MTV Spring Break?**

**What is the collective term for fans of The Wanted?**

**What do The Wanted have two of that fans have named after them?**

# WHY I HEART

Reading this annual is sure to have cemented your love for The Wanted. Now's your chance to write down exactly why they'll always be number one in your heart.

Feeling creative? Find a pencil and complete this cool acrostic poem. If you've never done one before, you simply use each of the vertical letters to begin each new horizontal line. Don't worry about rhyming, just have fun!

The Wanted will always be my most wanted because...

# THE WANTED

**T**............................................................................

**H**............................................................................

**E**............................................................................

**W**............................................................................

**A**............................................................................

**N**............................................................................

**T**............................................................................

**E**............................................................................

**D**............................................................................

# LATERS

Thanks for reading our annual and being party of the dedicated TWFanmily.
Keep rocking to our music during the year ahead and remember in the
meantime that we're never more than a click away!
For all our news & info check out our official website at www.thewantedmusic.com
or catch up with us via our dedicated YouTube channel.
Keep chatting on Twitter too, just visit www.twitter.com/thewantedmusic

To all our fans
Love

# ANSWERS

## THE BIG WANTED QUIZ
### PART 1 – TRUE OR FALSE

#### PAGES 24–25
1. False, it's Nathan.
2. False, Jay is from Newark, Nottingham shire. Tom is from Bolton.
3. True.
4. False, it's Jayne Collins
5. True.
6. False, it was 'All Time Low'.
7. True.
8. False, Jay is a vegetarian.
9. False, it's heights.
10. False, the band formed in 2009.

## WORDSEARCH
### PAGE 26

**AUDITION** is the extra word hiding in the grid.

#### PAGE 27
**The Boys And The Biebz**
1. Nathan
2. Jay
3. Max
4. Tom
5. Nathan
6. Jay, Max and Nathan.
Nathan even has a pet snake called Charlie.

#### PAGES 30–31
Who Said What?
1. Max
2. Siva
3. Nathan
4. Jay
5. Max
6. Jay
7. Siva
8. Jay
9. Tom
10. Nathan
11. Tom

#### PAGES 38–39
And The Award Goes To…
Nathan was crowned Best Celeb Tweeter by the Celebritain website.
Jay was named Sexiest Male Celeb Veggie by PETA, with Eliza Doolittle taking the female award.

#### PAGES 50–51
Who's Your Most Wanted?
Mostly a's  Masculine Max is your man.
Mostly b's  You and Jay are true lovebirds.
Mostly c's  You and Nathan would never run out of things to talk about.
Mostly d's  Sensitive Siva is just your type.
Mostly e's  Tom and you are a duet made in heaven.

## MISSING LYRICS

#### PAGES 52–53
**'LIGHTNING'**

pause
speak
chase
time

times
away from
skin
rush,

lips, kiss
frightening
might
time
frightening

Coats, room
teach
fear
clear

addicted
electric
comes

mine, life
little
lightning
know

skin, touch, kiss
rush
too
rush, rush